PERTURBATIONS

GARY BECK

Winter Goose
PUBLISHING
where words take flight

Winter Goose Publishing
45 Lafayette Road #114
North Hampton, NH 03862

www.wintergoosepublishing.com
Contact Information: info@wintergoosepublishing.com

Perturbations

First Edition, October 2017

Cover Design by Winter Goose Publishing
Typesetting by Odyssey Publishing

ISBN: 978-1-941058-70-1

Published in the United States of America

To Nancy,
whose bright spirit and charming wit
are a never-ending delight

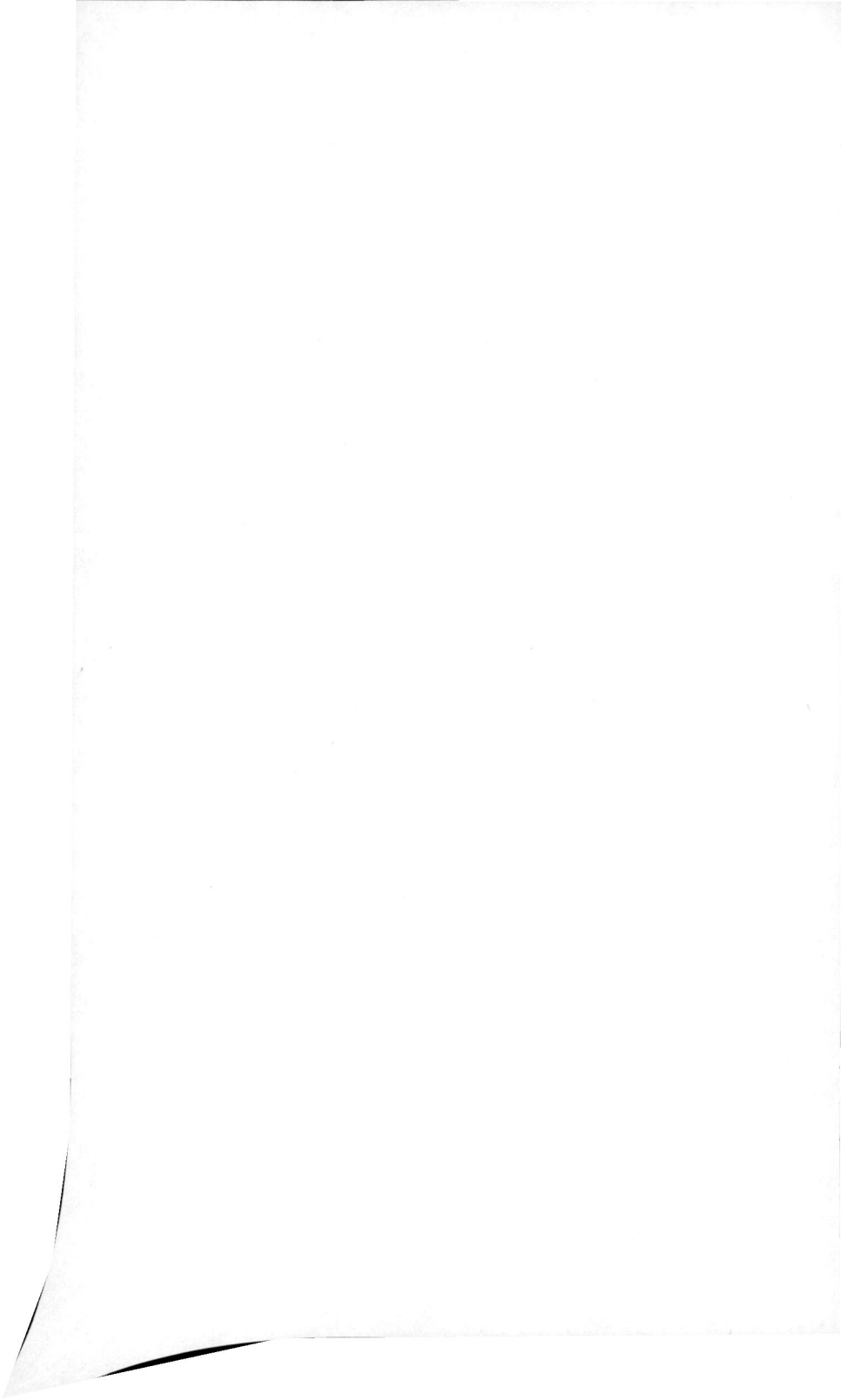

CONTENTS

"Patience, patience
Patience dans l'azur!
Chaque atome de silence
Est la chance d'un fruit mûr."

—Paul Valéry, "Palme"

Pledge

I pledged allegiance
when I was young,
to the flag
that seemed more substantial
than other country's flags,
to the republic for which it stands,
about which I knew nothing
except grade school mythology
purveyed by uninspired teachers,
of one nation, indivisible,
which seemed unrealistic
even at my credulous age,
with liberty and justice for all,
a conclusion I couldn't believe
despite urgent demands
to accept without questioning.

M,M,M, Mammon

As the Industrial Age
has given way
to the Information Age,
the dogs of law
have been unleashed
and bay of lawsuits
is a way of life.
So the tiny tail
wags the body politic,
encouraged by
scheming servants
of the lords of profit,
who lost trace elements
of humaneness,
bitterly achieved
in the struggle for survival,
as victims are prompted
to no longer mourn
the deaths of loved ones,
but to seek consolation
in the lawcourts.

Punishment Camp

Echo of evening song
in the restless night
as the last voices of complaint
serenade young campers
who toss on hard cots,
remembering harsh looks
of alien counselors
enriching the long summer.
Campers huddle in sparse shacks
courtesy of parents' generosity,
set against denuded hills,
polluted lake,
trapped in drowsiness,
still hungry,
the only hope,
escape in sleep.

Withdrawal

In a dazed variety of moments,
more lost than lover's separations,
I stretch one anguished, straining arm
not hard enough and slide again
into torpor and sexual fantasies.
The rest of me reposes,
silent and forgetful,
save for a tiny, mumbling voice
repeating over and over:
arise and save yourself
before immolation.

Lifer

Barred from taking flight,
an ancient eagle,
incurable wound gaping,
has surrendered its wings
that no longer compel the air
to curious spectators
who try to snatch a souvenir,
a once regal plume
that falls to the floor
of constricting cage
the zoo allows
to extinguish freedom.

Medical Visions

I heard a radio ad
that promised specialized treatment
in a hyperbaric chamber
for you or your loved ones
suffering from unhealed wounds.
Although I won't be here
for the miracle of inner healing,
if mankind survives itself
I have the fanciful hope
that someday science
will cure our ailments.

The Wonder of Birth

Children are stars
fallen from a dimness,
until the freedom thump,
clotted, yowling
stumbling from shelter,
greeted by older hands.
The child now delivered
from the last moments of security
wags its rubber feet,
screams its first protest
at the unheeding world.

Stuttgart Recollected

Remembered with a clarity,
a dervish-swirl vision,
the myth seen at midnight,
the mysterious Schlossplatz
and its castle of enchantment,
constructed before democracy.
The surrounding streets were silent,
but in the distance I could hear
the voices of American soldiers,
cursing, mostly in southern drawls,
and a mad cry rising above them,
the lament of a defeated relic,
raving in the night about Hitler:
"Adolf Hitler war mein freund,"
ignored by passersby
on the war-ravaged, rebuilt streets
of supine, resentful Germany,
that avoided total destruction
and allowed survivors
twisted by hopes of resurrection
to spin illusions of the past,
bewildering too many tomorrows
with convenient forgettings
that absolve the hills of Stuttgart
from renouncing beauty.

I remember one harsh night
sitting alone and broke
in the squalid Stuttgart Banhof,
hungry and fatigued,
without cigarettes or hope,
the after midnight drear
throttling my diminished expectations,
my soul eroded by failure,
as I sat at comfortless table
listening to the German waiters
talk to the Italian untermenschen
as if they were children.

One brash young Italian,
resplendent in a flannel shirt,
bounced buoyantly
around the waiting room
babbling to anyone who noticed
in his search for attention.
He pranced and posed
for a tired, aging whore
sitting with his countrymen,
hoping for late night business.
He smiled, sneered, snickered
in sly pursuit that she ignored,
scorning his childish allure,
but no one else responded,
so she left with him.

I no longer know
if the wind still blows the leaves
along the sculpted paths
of Stuttgart schloss,
slick with winter frost
covering the pools where goldfish swam
in more peaceful times,
now abandoned for warmer climes,
leaving turgid, tarnished water
beneath the frigid surface
that cannot compel
the brief day's sunlight
to oblige the palace
with the thaw of spring.

Shattered

When love has departed
and bitter dreams remain,
I think of midnight meetings
as we groped like deaflings
eager to touch each other,
until there was no more past.
Tonight a scorching pang
isolates the lost weavers
crushing the hope of intertwine,
the shuttle of our joining.

The goat god plays his mocking pipes,
my feet move in the ancient dance,
but my heart is as stone as statue.
I sit beside the turmoil pool
and watch the last angels
bow their heads in finality
as the frigid moon passes by
and my love is deceased.

Retrieved Moments

How strange to meet the past,
as idle as a sensual spider
flicking arms of whimsy
for the new day's destiny
that captures us again
coursing streets of passion,
building pyres of ambition.
Suddenly, as if the past
were opening a torpid eye
of human interference,
someone we once knew
is shunted before us
raising the specter of old visions.
The moment's pause,
strained words of greeting,
then a relieved farewell,
but later the revelation
that the tendrils of time
spin despite us.

Shock

I say one final word
then we part
and sagging from sorrow,
though part we must,
I walk the hurricane night
unable to touch anyone,
unable to find rest.
My pathetic laments
echo the same cries
of every solitary child
pained and bewildered
by the loss of love.

Last Stop

I sit beside you on the subway
and know from your look
that love is gone.
Still I court the chimneysweep's daughter,
who wears an imitation fur collar,
whiter than her tainted soul.
I did not hope for miracles,
expect to part seas, walk on water,
in the age of doubt
and I anticipated nothing.
Then you stood up with
your surprising thighs,
passed me like a woman strutting
before the passenger's approving eyes
as I felt stripped naked,
bared to the glances of strangers,
and hid behind a newspaper shield,
whose sheets of violence
were mere reflections
of the carnivorous world.
As we neared the final station
I cautiously looked at my fellow riders,
whose eyes instantly
turned to advertisements
that concealed them from my anguish.

Instant Attraction

One brief glance
for a fleeting moment
in a rain-stormed city,
struck with the frenzy
of a mugger's knife
gutting the shell
of a concealed heart.
I spilled incoherent words,
like marbles falling from a child's pocket
tumbling wildly, out of control.
I was possessed
and passion gripped me
like insistent hands on an udder.
She jumped into a taxi
frightened or annoyed
and ignored my plea to wait.
I stood helplessly on the sidewalk
wiping the rain from my face,
too stunned to find shelter,
and watched her become
another lost moment.

Misinterpretations

The zookeeper throws a slab of meat
to the caged king,
who watches like a beggar,
but dreams he made a gory kill.

So my dreams
have become torments
that no longer give respite
from delusive expectations.

Inadvertent Seer

Once upon a long ago,
in the Bowery, now forgotten,
I met an ancient derelict.
He staggered to me,
hand outstretched,
craggy fingers winking,
screamed:
"Ten cents for the secret to success."
I gave him a quarter
and he turned to go,
twitching in anticipation
of a quarter's blind escape.
"Your secret please," I said.
He led me to a tenement,
after I took a vow of silence,
and showed me rows of empty bottles.
I was perplexed.
"What does it mean?" I asked.
"Resist much. Obey little," he replied,
"or you'll end up like me,
consumed by wanting."
This meant nothing to me
and I watched him seep away,
absorbed by the cracked floor.

Function

Voice of mad, exuberant spring,
the whole world dreams
eagerly pollinating
while I sit upon depression bed
and cannot join the revels.
The first bumble bee smiles at me
and I forget my dreary sorrow
as I enjoy the improbable flight
of another servant of nature
more specialized then I,
too busy to waste time brooding
about trivial causality.

Evolved Mating

Yes, my new-found love,
you penetrated me
and though I tried to keep you out
with the finality of a woman's closed
thighs,
you forced your rude entry,
a torturous assault,
full of obscene commotion,
a little boy yelling obscenities.
Now tonight you sleep beside me
sated, mewling, hand on crotch,
not that far removed from Og
and sex in survival cave.

Remote Companions

My neighbors' faces are closed doors
and their forbidden apartments
leak sounds of mysterious events.
It is hopeless to expect invitations.
Footsteps, voices, laughter,
the smells of cooking
declare themselves foreign.
It is hard to imagine
that they may have
the same hungers,
the same torments
confusing my days.

Dream Omens

The solitary visions of a man
who never sees joy in other faces,
but feels their unendurable pain,
as they are poised at the implacable gate
that opens on survival, or doom.
Billions cluster in the grip of indecision.
How hard for us to choose
and if we live the myth of others
and use lust to blunt our souls,
our hunger will crush our dreams
that grow too weak for striving.

Construction Site

Shall our love
that claws us
like jungle savages,
rending flesh and soul,
shatter and be denied
because we don't have time
to lick each other's wounds?
Shall we be so busy
sucking on the universe
that we forget
tumescent evenings
when your glow lit the night,
languid mornings
when naked,
twined like sleeping serpents,
we stirred like cuddly children
and sailed off to dreams?
Shall I tell myself
my hands have never touched
the softness of your hips,
my mouth the aphrodisiac of your lips,
when they have learned to fit you?
Should we accept
that lover's insecurity
dooms continuations.

Common Sparrow

Fly darling,
wings more hesitant than a baby sparrow.
I will catch you if you fall.
I listened to your chirping
as you lay close and clinging
in the wrinkled midnight of your sheets,
lonely, lost, afraid.
I passed my hand
across the smoothness
of your freckled back,
soothing you,
your legs curled
like tiny lizards in the sun,
basking in sleep
in the comforting nest.

Bankrupt

The children of man,
blind-spilled upon the earth,
are lost, wasted,
devoured by
the cruel seas they sail
to school, home, play.
They are bred to be fed
to the belly of Moloch,
allocated to destruction
for the sin of consuming,
consigned without choice
to a fate that cash or credit
will not avert.

Another Voyage

When I was young I heard a voice
that whispered to me in the night
saying that soon I would die.
For many years I walked in fear,
seeing myself expired on a lonely shore,
my only memorial
a slaughtered whale's tooth.
But those days passed.
I shed the distant dread
of vultured deserts.
Soon the wondrous journey ends,
a caravan's safe arrival
at a welcoming city,
eternal torment, nothingness, waiting,
I know not what, but cultivate acceptance.

Accused

Nature is not cruel, but just,
and though we tremble at judgement
there must be a vision
of enduring todays,
rebuilding tomorrows.
Nature never cast a benevolent eye,
nor had patience with our efforts
that consumed the bounty of the earth.
As our inexorable trials approach,
there will not be mercy
for the innocent or guilty.

For Man Who Dies

The man who pits himself
against dread time
to make some imprint on the book of life
is snuffed out briefly,
like a short-lived spark
and tastes the futile nothingness of death.
Yet death sometimes tastes of defeat,
for in each age for those who died
the living cherish a remembered flame
and memory outlives the tomb.

What I Would Like to Find One Day When Opening a *Wall Street Journal*

Attention investors:
watch fish carefully.
Brains may be in style
again.

(AP) A tom cat was found gorging
himself in a tuna cannery. Just
before he died from overeating,
he was heard to mumble: my
people will triumph.

Alaska. Dangerous men still trade
in brain dust and many turned-up
toes, toted to the worms (of napkins
in their laps) whisper the legend of
the lost grey matter mine.

Wire Service:
Upholding Sherman Anti-Trust
precedents, the World Court ruled that the search for
the sons
of Moby Dick must cease.

Marine biologists have discovered communication among
sharks and have revealed their plan to come ashore and live with humans.

River's Edge

My love is a strand of hair
gleaming on my sweater.
Nothing else remains.
She left me for another.
I sit alone by the East River
and far away,
fading into darkness,
a distant light of a ship flickers,
its foghorn breaks the silence
with a piercing wail
that is my song,
merges swiftly with city clamor,
quickly disappears,
lost in midnight current.

Infliction

When blind fear
carried by an urgent cry
turns another hope of refuge
into a chamber of despair
I cannot find comfort
in my self of isolation.
My thoughts are deadly curses,
crushing all who thwart me,
yet they circle my ambivalent globe
and return as my burden.

Lost Road

Weary me and sullen you
as the night grows old
our search back to each other
becomes more difficult, more cold.
The last heart has only one pulse
and dissension shall sever us.
If I never sleep and have the dream
and spend your nights in bitter myth,
strained fingers creeping over braille,
touch will never be our resolution.
The midnight harpist strums,
plucking a lover's melody
and I sing alone,
while the plaster Buddha on the mantel
broods and may or may not pray.

Doggie Days

I saw two puppies play
in the momentarily safe
green escape of Central Park.
They did not know
hazards of this tortured life,
rampant perils lurking
behind every door,
on any corner,
so their carefree frolic
in the ancient doggie game
of challenge, run, mock fight,
was merely a respite
from burdens to come.

Alienation

I lie alone
upon a naked bed
and twist the darkness
into executioners
dancing 'round the suppurations
of my leper love.
I am a castaway
in a cannibal world
and make forays for sustenance,
always looking behind me.
Every tense moment
a hazardous expedition
as I go forth unarmed,
having sheathed my sword
to subtract one combatant
from this holocaust life,
finding the mob rabid,
am forced to hide
in feral anonymity,
compelled to accept
life's torturous condition.

Hard Heart

Where are you, woman,
while I sit in lonely silence
in a loveless room?
Are you sleeping,
while I pace the fraying borders
of my prison room?
Vintage thoughts of you pierce the night.
Do you twist and turn at night,
restless for someone who is not there?
No. Not you.
You sleep the sleep of the just,
but are neither just nor virtuous.
I guess everyone sleeps,
except me.
Why?
Have I committed
some nauseating crime
that you should sleep
night after night,
while I grip my sheets in frenzy,
tear the blanket in desperation,
gnash my teeth into the pillow,
lubricate the bed with sullen sweat?
Will I ever find one night
of inconsequential sleep?

Sanctuary

The violation of my apartment,
my substitute womb,
where I take refuge in a secret haven,
has been disrupted by intruders
into my dream, my chamber of safety.
The greedy fingers of despoliation
didn't pillage everything,
leaving garments that I never earned,
liquor that should be renounced,
an ancient dagger, toy of fools and me,
other objects, worthless things.
I cannot visualize the rapers of my privacy,
faces, race, color, ethnicity.
These nameless shadows of intrusion
did not touch my poems,
my dread or fantasy
that some hand of envy or spite,
in a wanton, malicious moment
would destroy my poems.
So if the erratic hand of justice
seizes the thieves
by some coincidence,
perhaps there will be mercy
since they didn't do their worst.

Fateful Moment

Our eyes met,
a mute coincidence
that suddenly promised
a lavish feast
for famished children.
We cautiously approached,
serpents compelling each other
to a dangerous dance
that enticed us closer.
Then hostile faces frightened her
and she fled my invitation.
I tried to follow her,
but taloned fingers grasped me
and would not relent,
then she was gone
and would not come again.

Awakenings

Asleep in a garden I lay
and the sun rose,
warming my body
with nourishing heat.
When I awakened
death's chill had passed
and I went forth
into the desert,
filled with great strength.
Suddenly I knew
that death is powerless
over sleeping men
and only in the frenzy
of the streets of life
will time's servant labor
and collect his due.

Future Hopes

Our land, where innocence has lingered
too long, an innocent fingered,
degraded by the smut
of mouths and hands
that deflowered their own selves,
betrayed their frightened neighbors.
My visions not patriotic visions,
but attained pride of survivals,
confronted in power plots of rivals,
gnawed at by our friend's intentions,
confused and weakened by inventions,
flowing for some in abundance . . .
In war . . . Disorder . . .
We who shall not surrender
this dreamland hope of tomorrow,
the often forgotten testimony
that is our inherited creation, America,
shall not let the voices of destruction
that cry in newsprint for yieldings,
that caw on the airwaves praising foes,
that whine and mewl in the forum,
blind to threats of obliteration
from those who promise to destroy us.
Deceived by enemies, enticed by friends,

America shall endure and outlast
the fearful and treacherous among us,
ready to erode without contest
the unspoken pride of pulse
that is our nation, our endeavor.

Endurance

Trapped in sultry nights,
slave to my senses,
wandering through effigies of lust,
the incoherent singer crazed on self,
a hungry addict of expansion,
peopling an emptiness . . .
A dream . . . A ghosting . . . A forever incomplete.
Dazed in a wilderness of imagination
trees become walls,
the grass playthings of rootless feet.
I lift an unyielding voice
crying of children to come.
Old visions scarcely remembered,
fugitive and fleeting,
we believe in arrival.
Tents on the desert are struck
and prophets are awaited.
The harbors are filled
with the comings of strangers
and streets of stone
leave no trace of passing.
We sit in the stillness
of rooms in the cities
surrounded by swirls of a violent breeder.

We pace in the silence
of homes in the towns
fevered with anguish
for change and commotion.
We are the fruits of ancient despoiling
the limbless creation
of sires and grandsires
still daring to shout defiance
at those who would consume us

Redemption: In Memory of William Blake

In the visions of the seer
who foretells the future dire
flaming hands of God appear
with a scourge of holy fire.

To eliminate from earth
since compassion's painful flight
human hatred there since birth
that is persecuting light,

which with rays of blessed love
and with purpose unallayed
will become the one above
and forget the hell they made.

In Flight

This creature in the air
in chairs of comfort
is mankind,
who out of ancient ooze
dragged his body
till he stood erect,
contemplated his past path
and dreamed of the stars.

Vow

If walls around me I must have
let me build them with my own hands.
I shall not to crushing prison
lead myself,
unless the fetters fixed on me
are placed
by my erring self.

Past Yearnings

I have lain beside soft women,
kissed their flesh, touched their hair,
have seen their eyes, locked tight in love
afterwards, grow blank, then stare,
trapped in an ancient yearning spell,
some thought of youth, some faded hope,
and never to another tell
what dwindling promise lingered there.

Social Revolutionary

Dark angels burning
as I sit propped against a teakwood wall
listening to women chatter,
conversation of no matter.
Savage shadows flickering by firelight
as I sit cramped within a wedgewood hall
listening to teacups clinking,
perfumed armpits stinking.
Tigers stalking in the night
as I sit waiting for the eagle's call
watching virgins shatter,
hot thighs flatter.
Wild voices crying in the night
as I sit hoping for the tyrant's fall
hare-lipped matrons slinking,
abandoned wives shrinking.
Then tired of useless talk,
impotent protest
I seek liberating sleep.

Transported

I sing a poem of love
inspired by your cello voice
that leaves my insides tingly
and find myself fluted
by Ionic columns,
to temples of elation.

Serenade

Mighty strains of music lift my spirit
and I feel sweet chilling tingles
of ecstatic wonder
up and down my frame.
Within my breast
vast oceans surge and foam,
heavens split asunder, fall,
and gods of man's rich fantasy
moan and whine to see their doom.
Oh lustful Zeus, and gentle Christ,
wise, meek Buddha
and learned Kung Fu Tze,
Odin does outlive you all
within my mind.
A god who though his end is near
spent his eye for wisdom dear,
who though most noble
will also pass within the current
of orchestral sound.

Short Lament

Who hungers for the world
hungers with me
and hears the world cry
louder than me.

Renunciation

In the evening of despair
while the fruitless sit and mourn
for the god who does not care
how the living shall be bourne
to the sound of painful dirge
down the hallway of release
from life's sinews to emerge
and renounce the hope of peace.

Precious Poets

Pour forth
from the tempestuous torrent
of bitter loathing
undying combat
against fetid workers of speech,
whose endless self-styled flow
of effete rhetoric
assails the portals
of the self of isolation
to drag and thrust us
into the eternal sty.

Vulnerable

Tears descend
like a raging sandstorm,
whipping, stinging,
catching me unprotected
in the desert of love.

Progress

Long did the fires
burn above Troy,
the flames' ravages
lighting the night.
The cries of widows and orphans,
the shrieking laments
of desolate mothers,
young maidens pursued
by relentless Achaeans,
the swirl of battle
within Priam's walls,
the desperate Trojans
falling by sword and by spear,
fighting in vain for their city,
another page of destruction
in the annals of civilization.

Self-Portrait

I eat, sleep, am nourished
by unspiritual opportunities,
am anticipated in my desertions,
find no roadside shrine
that strengthens me,
made mostly of long bones,
dwindling enchantments,
still nurturing hopes
for endurable survival.

Parental Illusions

In every man
the little part, still boy,
holds desperate illusions
however base,
that once, in youth,
loved and cherished
by a father's strength,
a mother's soft caress,
there was a citadel
to nurse one's wounds.
This tiny place of roots
though puny, fickle refuge,
haven in despair,
held puissant awe
until demanded.
Then locking one out
(temple doors denying the defiler)
that self of need
wove strange, unreal myths
remembered as the past.

No Rest

The light of cities
invades the night,
smashes the hope
of beleaguered Mother Nature
to recuperate
from man's assault.

Night Shift

In the omitted hours of existence,
a man, forlorn but not forgotten,
rides the solitary subway.
He has the pasty face
of night shift,
peering over the feeble body
of the city-dweller.
Home to sleep, perchance to dream
about desire
in tired, overworked images,
used often
in flights of hectic fantasy
away
from painful night-shift.

Lost Search

I sat within myself one day
and saw my spirit rise
and weave a blade of searing fire
before my sleeping eyes.
I felt my weary mind awake
and cast off fetters deep
and leave the cell my thoughts had made
with manacles of sleep.
I looked with famished eyes and ears
for signs that I could trust,
but all I found was sad deceit
that turned my hopes to dust.

Forlorn

I shall feel free
when night comes softly
with its magic, into me,
to cry aloud to unseen listeners
of my sorrow and despair.
For often I have cried out
that I am still strong,
have become old, wise,
and only in aloneness lost
admitted weakness of my spirit.

Mad Seeker

A prophet-wanderer crazed on self,
too long scaling cloud-hid mountains,
came into the fields of man
singing the roots of creation,
that slim-child tree
nourished by the blood of altars,
but found no listeners,
and preached desolately,
until he was stoned to death.

Missing

Often in the midnight silence
I wander a desolate path
along the East River.
I lean on the dank, frigid railing
that bars me from the river
and listen to the night-noise.
A chugging tug-boat
pulling heavy-laden barges
rends the night
with its whistle's plaintive screech,
while I watch the river
flowing to the sea
and remember you.

Isolation

If the world is cruel and strange
never sing,
for song is a carnal sorrow.
Goddess of my midnight visions
listening to the last song,
my only audience
in this harsh life
of inattention.

Fragile Span

The living moment of the world
comes, a dark tide of oppression,
heavy, gravitic, pulling the hope of life
down, down,
content to feed on ebbing dreams,
as resistance fades
from feeble expectation.

Inaction

Indelible dream
planted deeper than a farmer's seed,
I water you with words
and watch you slowly die.
I should labor as quenching rain,
instead I waste myself in talk
and shatter the cage of silence
as I pace from wall to wall
and the parched vision shrivels.

Education

To grow
in vast fields of funereal stones
that whisper in sodden murmurs,
in gathering dusk,
to frogs that croak and chant
the ancient epic lays
that no longer console
our fractured youth.

Irritation

For the betterment
and to propagate the fertility
of my soul,
I shall have you imprisoned
in a fashionable mortuary,
stuff you with cardboard,
fill your veins with lava
and watch your bones
ferment into motor oil.
You bore me effortlessly,
efficaciously,
a dreary vehicle,
driving me to despair.

Brief Vision

Once in a dream-like vision
familiar to the seer
I saw atop a mountain
the hand of God appear
within the storm-tossed heavens
and brush the clouds away
quell the noisy thunder
and reveal the light of day

Au Natural

We always walk in the shadow
of something, someone
and don't know
what, who,
or care to believe,
or dare to act.

In the shadow of time,
personal catastrophes
are not more terrifying
than nature's cataclysms.

Whims

The spawning world is near
and will more than sow the seeds,
fetid, blasted with corrosion
that contain the lust I fear.
The day's expenditure, perversions,
coursing the brief meetings,
partings wordless and regretted,
affairs to tend, diversions.

Sociology

People of my land
I cry:
I am not so fine as you.
The dull faces
and slow limbs
moving the mornings,
mocked by strange motions
are sullen quitters
of grey scowl afternoons,
but don't represent
our better yearnings.

Peeper

I have watched you late at night,
in your secret chamber of dreams,
as you bared your Park Avenue thighs,
stretched before my wondering eyes,
pressed two tiny fists
against your winking breasts,
then turned off the light
and denied me delight.

Brief Love

Love,
one season,
shed like serpent's skin,
mouldering in memory
of remote forests.
One season, young serpent.
Will a new skin come again?
Will love caress
like snakes twining on saplings,
unconcerned with the future?

Oppression

For you will this forever last?
This particle of love's coarse flame
that sweeps us from our bitter past
to rhythms of our sterile game.

Your spring, aspects of motion,
cycling change of season,
fingering a sullen notion,
love, deny me my unreason.

Sing not patriotic fervor
cruel men live master to server,
hands pluck a ballot from another
heap throttling chains on their brother.

Fable

When elephants walked upright
and birds swam in the sea,
I met a little osprey
and he told this tale to me:
Ten thousand, thousand years ago
man rose from beds of slime
and made all animals his foe
and gave birth to dread time.

Enigma

If glory is a futile lust
and duty is the path we must
pursue, what of our dreaming then,
the whimpering of fearful men?
Resolute and knowledged in defy
we arm and seek the senseless fray,
step-child of our arrogant display,
and dispute the sense of how and why.
Then desire, doomed by its own intent,
an emanation, gut-hot, by another sent
into exile, to rot without a trace,
till it reappears in a kinder place.

Brief Encounter

If you are not more real
then three days of brief imagining,
how long is a dream?
You have come
out of an unknown vista,
from a world I do not know
of endless privilege,
denied to sons of poverty.

Now carried by a happy river
to a distant, luxury shore,
you preen yourself
on guarded decks
that insure immunity
from crude importunity.

Nature's Promise

When din of earthly sounds appall
and all my spirit finds is sorrow,
then I shall remember
my strange, serene sojourn
in a battered shack, on a flowered cliff
by the roaring sea.
There, when I sat in thundering stillness
and first began to know the sea,
I heard the ancient ocean call:
"Join me when your days are done."
And I, in ignorance cried out:
"Why can't I descend into your depths?
Now when my strength still surges
and I wish to sound your mysteries,
I am not welcome."
Then I heard a calming voice:
"Patience. Mortal.
There are still tasks to be done."

Infatuation

Nothing held more promise
than the meeting of our eyes,
like hungry children staring at a feast.
Two serpents compelling each other,
we glided until we intertwined
and doing the same dance,
though strangers to each other's flesh,
we drew closer than copulation.
Suddenly ringed by hostile, flabby faces
she grew afraid and fled.
I tried to follow.
Taloned fingers held me.
She was gone and never would return,
but brief desire won't be forgotten.

Man's Hope

To the spirit of man in the night
who vigils of loneliness keeps,
between moments of deep innersight
of frail brothers for whom he weeps.
For sorrows that breed in the span
that truth and love do last
in the weary spirit of man,
until his desire has passed.
Then in the self new-born
a marvelous hope is bared
that dreams will not be outworn,
as long as visions are shared.

Consumed

A last death only comes
when days and nights have passed
with funerals of dreams
fading in a black procession
until I am left alone,
my love turned cannibal,
feasting on my waning strength,
striking at me more than evil
in this conspiring world.

Visions of Man

Never seeing joy,
but crying at the unendurable,
we have no brothers
when trapped in ourselves.
We stand poised at the implacable gate,
but few go in and few remain outside,
as billions cluster at the wall of indecision.
How hard to choose
and if we stand with others
and live their myth
and live on pain that blinds
and our lust hides our souls,
we will not sate hunger
by merely wishing.

Another Loss

The long, hungry stride of time
traps us in the cave of darkness,
with memory our sole companion,
as we watch with famished eyes
a lovely maiden who we potently desire
pass and be lost
in the vast man-tide
that swallows strangers.

Recycle

When the world's no longer with us
and dread things will cease to be,
great pain will change to pleasure
and great joy will terrify.
Then life will breed grim chaos
until once again renewed
and a better breed aspires
to tend out battered earth.

Questions of Youth

What is a boy? What does he dream? What does he
hunger for?
Is he just a groping whirl
of atoms, lying, blushing, visioning? Does he seek a love
that's only sung in ancient
books? Does he seek a father who was never there? A
mother active in the PTA?
Is he some random product of a night that was repented?
Some blind spasmic habit of creation? A seed of love,
faded, lurking in a photo album, a red withered rose,
crushed between the pages.

Is he a night child, lost to darkness, full of frenzy and
despair, losing youth in a constant plea for some atten-
tion . . . ? Any attention? He plays, he fights, he studies,
he sulks and will not eat his meals. He tastes forbidden
treasures of the adult life with other boys,
fumbles through the mysteries with an adventurous girl.

Six, twelve, eighteen, what is he? Is the hot blaze of
fantasy behind a pimpled forehead ever known? Are
the burning flushes of desire behind a gawky smile ever
seen? Is the mad song of drunken poet, fervid lover, dar-
ing hero, stuttered in self-conscious words, ever heard?

He passes in an unnoticed haze, churning the current of
his life. His path's constrained, his thoughts are given.
All but the secret soul that is a boy is known. In his
isolation, he is
the last dream.

Dare I

Silence flutters, moth in flame
consumed by hesitation.
Shall I speak, or shall I shriek?
Shall I stare at cracking plaster walls,
or flute the words at another
and risk that painful state,
final rejection?

Continued Hope

O passionate designer
there is no denying
that we are consuming tomorrows.
Our sun burns brightly
and we have no remembrance of sorrow.
We shall praise each other
until our day's delight is done,
then perishing old desires,
make new journeys.

Hopeless Plea

In the night,
where sorrow and the lost sit,
forever hiding from the thoughts
denied by day's wisdom,
we invoke weak pleas,
murmuring of spirits
that once trod the earth
in realms of fantasy,
yearning for a savior.

Mon Amour

You who have given me
your sweet lips
and made no measure
of the loving gift
that brought me pleasure,
are cherished beyond forgetting
in everyday renewal.

Imminent Despair

This bloom of decay,
hanging a smothering blanket
over my crumbling world,
my poorly-built soul
no longer sustaining
heart felt visions
for suffering mankind,
hope for the future
dissolving swiftly
from the assault of greed.

Defeat

In the fierce pattern of struggle days,
youth proud, stuffed with lore,
dauntless, confident, supreme,
awakens one sullen morning,
crippled, strength fled, wingless,
unable to seek refuge,
crushed by another rejection.

Historical Regret

Between the feeling and the word
the bleeding world lies lifeless,
weakened by understanding and speech,
expressions of our civilized state,
no longer primitive and unconquered.

Inured

In my days of earthly sorrow
I tell my spirit be serene.
Soon there comes the dread tomorrow
and after that I won't be seen.
For in the blaze of freedom
I quench my burning thirst,
forget the earthly kingdom
which tempts me to my worst.

Backward Glimpse

A poem is often sadder than farewell
to a moderately cared-for loved one.
There is no softening romantic haze,
just slight sorrow and forgetful ease.
Love to the cultured may be a poem,
piercing through the span of recollections,
summoning distant memories of joy,
buried moments of misery
stored somewhere in the brain's core,
a dormant vision not readily remembered,
separated by the vague image of a lover,
never incandescent, but awakening.

Weary Unto . . .

We who have dared to wage
the war of youth,
the slothful, weary dreamers
blind to truth,
the lost men visioning a sad parade,
that replaced the hope of an accolade.
We who have dedicatedly reclined
upon a couch of sloth and weak despair,
discovered our true virtues have declined,
abandoned us in the midst of nowhere.

Apprehensions

When we are blinded by fear
of known or unknown tomorrows,
preparing fulfillments to be lost
before they're reached,
in rigorous paths of denial
that leave us with corruption,
the gift of inaction.

Rental

The pigeon's frantic flutters
against the doors and shutters
of an ancient, broken house
where a cranky woman mutters,
drives tranquility away,
spreads an aura of decay,
that ends the new tenant's hopes
to bring in the light of day.

Paradox

Blueberries and rape,
hummingbirds and persecution,
Pi and chaos,
contradictions seem to be
the very core of mystery,
for within them is contained
the good and evil in mankind.

Artifact

Forge a blade in purest fire
from finest steel and shape it.
Hammer it to hardness, then
let it cool and pound again,
until the truest sword is done.
Then, a worthy hand to find
to wield a warrior's weapon,
until gunpowder ends its rule.

Idle Fantasy

Barely making ghostly contact
in a meeting soon forgotten,
leaving me lusting the supine eruption
of endurable conjoinment
with your soft flesh.

Balkan Turmoil

They walk an earth
of arrogance and treachery
convinced of an evil vision,
torturing others,
condemning their brothers,
cursing different religions,
hating different ethnics.
This Ottoman inheritance,
indolent and corrupt,
aggravated by Hapsburg greed,
fueled by nationalistic fantasies,
bestows gifts of bitterness and blood
century after century
that will only be ended by globalism.

Aspiration

Though I no longer throb with visions
for the betterment of mankind,
my passions have not released me
from hope
and clamoring with rebukes
for my neglect
my finer self hungers for tomorrow.

Frail Bird

Tiny sparrow
hiding from other sparrows
in the briars of your nest,
hear a prophecy:
the silken buzzard
lures with sweet delights,
cotton candy,
clinks of golden coin,
but to fly with buzzards
you must be one.
When you lie at night,
crooning on my covering wing,
your taut wings shatter,
swallow your overwhelming chatter
that makes you lose
nourishment from your greedy beak.
You crawl into the comfort
of my warming feathers,
though you clawed them in the day.
Sparrow, full of fear,
I wipe the blood your talons drew . . .
and hold you near.

Material Gains

Miami Beach glitter,
Collins Avenue Friday night,
far west crescent moon,
storm cloud shroud
spread by lightning,
Venus above, passing serene
over human strife.
SUVs, BMWs,
alien pauses
of damaged values.

Dreary Days

The voice of time
forever speaks in the dark,
when I am sick of dreams
and more procrastination.
If I could calm the dark hatred
and endure my final spring,
despite no rejoicing
I may survive tomorrow.

No Eulogy, This

Tonight, a poet sits,
somewhere in his lonely world,
while reflections pass
of love for his country,
yet reviled, spurned.
This man dared assault
the rulers of his nation
who conceal the evils he endures.
No place for love
when force prevails.
His fate? I know not,
yet I realize
the world does not weep for him.

Distances

Often thwarted by reality
which has little kindness for error,
making me remember
visions of tomorrow
that always exclude me
from touching another,
for I am past redeeming,
and more cannot be expected.

Quick Trip

When to another's luring song
your brief devotion suddenly strays,
am I better off than before?
No longer a child of visions,
my dreams feature no tomorrows,
only the daily fear remains
transubstantiated into stolidity.
Then I get old,
waiting for my life to pass,
and I grow cold,
fearing that nothing will last.
So do not begin with remembrances,
contorted by passion's frenzy
that will distort perception,
for the sphere of earth spins slower,
the affairs of man are more desperate
and my time speeds by, relentless.

Used Poets

Tongue-licking words,
mere sugar coating
of iniquities, dagger strikes
of helpless poets,
heat gone, toothless remains,
weary of past songs,
blinded by visions of freedom,
that will soon be forgotten
in electronic tomorrows.

Street Trade

Down time-worn streets
where lonely harlots roam
the empty night of no trade,
turned cannibal by consuming dread
of approaching hunters
who will allow predation
to devour us all.

Brooklyn, 1776

We won't suicide desire
in the graveyards of retreat,
permit future hopes to tire
and fade from our grim defeat.
We will march another day
and confront our former friends
till the bloodstains fade away
and the thought of conflict ends.

Learning Scale

Long addicted to ancient languages
that preserved the voices of time,
countless cultures rising and falling.
Greece. Rome. Byzantium.
Where are they?
The survival struggle of ideas
have elevated the soul of man,
who still behaves,
despite their nourishment,
like savages of old.

Poems from *Perturbations* have appeared in: *Bibliotheca Alexandrina, Blast Furnace Press, Blue Bonnet Review, Bohemian Pupil Press, Bright Light Café/Bright Light Multimedia, Corvus Review, Defunct, Exercise Bowler, Green's Magazine, Grey Book Press, Hypertext Magazine, Innovate Magazine, Literary Brushstrokes, Literary Lunes, Miller's Pond Poetry Magazine (H&H Press), Momoware (Gray Book Press), Nazar Look, Original-Writers.com/Writers Haven, Page & Spine, Pink Eye Lemonade, See Spot Run, Spank the Carp, The Bond Street Review (Ink Publications), The Golden Lantern (Hip Pocket Press), The Greensilk Journal, The Legendary, The Mayo Review, The Stray Branch, Time Zones Lit Review, Title Publishing House, Vagabondage Press, Word Salad Poetry Magazine, Writers Haven Magazine,* and *Verseland.*

About the Author

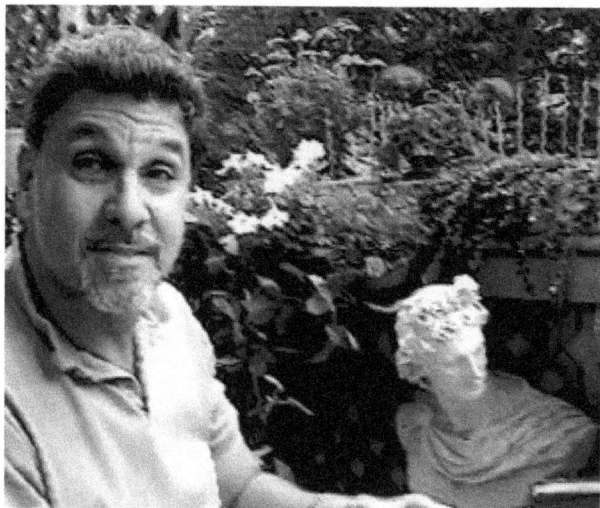

Gary Beck has spent most of his adult life as a theater director. He has had numerous published works including *Days of Destruction, Expectations,* and his novel, *Call to Valor,* published by Gnome On Pig Productions. Gary has also had several original plays and translations produced off Broadway, in New York City, where he currently resides.

www.ingramcontent.com/pod-product-compliance
Lightning Source LLC
Chambersburg PA
CBHW051732040426
42447CB00008B/1093